27

Keys To A
Successful
Marriage

KEVIN A TREASURE

27 KEYS TO A SUCCESSFUL MARRIAGE
Copyright © 2014 by Decisions Determine Destiny Press

Decisions Determine Destiny Press

Ordering Information:
Quantity sales. Special discounts are available on quantity purchases by corporations, associations, and others. For details, contact the publisher at the address above.
Orders by U.K. trade bookstores and wholesalers. Please contact Kevin Treasure:

Mob: 07903 940 399
Email: kevintreasure@gmail.com
Website: www.kevintreasure.com

First Edition 2014

ISBN: 978-0-9927831-2-9

Dedication

To my beautiful wife Michelle,
who also happens to be my best friend,
my children,
Kevelle, Keturah and Kezzia.

TABLE OF CONTENTS

INTRODUCTION

A wedding is one of life's great moments, a time of solemn commitment of love between a man and a woman.

Marriage is intended by God to be a creative relationship, as his blessing enables husband and wife to love and support each other in good times and in bad, and to share in the care and upbringing of children. It is based upon a solemn, public and lifelong covenant between a man and a woman, declared and celebrated in the presence of God and before witnesses.

The 27 Keys To A Successful Marriage is your guide to the good life. Your marriage is intended to be lasting, enjoying and special, the expression of love between a man and a woman. It has its ups and downs, and it won't always be easy but applying the keys in this book your marriage can be a beautiful union between you and your spouse. Learn how to make your spouse your best friend and enjoy the marriage you have.

Love is patient; love is kind; love is not envious or boastful or arrogant or rude. It does not insist on its own way; it is not irritable or resentful; it does not rejoice in wrongdoing, but rejoices in the truth. It bears all things, believes all things, hopes all things, endures all things.
– 1 Corinthians 13.4-7 –

1

COMMUNICATION

It is often said that Communication is the Key. So talk to each other...Often, about everything. You'll know what's in your spouse's heart by what comes out their mouth.

Communication to a relationship is like Oxygen to life, without it, it Dies.
– Tony Gaskins –

2

SELF EXAMINATION

You are not always right, try and step back and view things from your spouse's point of view, do unto others as you would have them do unto you.

Many marriages would be better if the husband and the wife clearly understood that they are on the same side.
– Zig Ziglar –

3

HONESTY

Be honest and open with each other you'll be surprised what you'll learn from being honest. Learn to voice your opinions in a constructive way that leads to a constructive outcome.

Being honest may not get you a lot of friends but it'll always get you the right ones.

4

APOLOGISE

Apologises, when you need to and when you are wrong, to keep the peace. Your spouse does not always have to be the first to apologise. When you develop an attitude of never being the first to apologise it creates frustration in your spouse.

Nowhere in the Bible does it say that we should wait for someone else to do the right thing before we do the right thing.
– Sheila Wray Gregoire –

5

INTEGRITY

Never talk behind each others back to other people. It creates mis-trust, hurts feelings and causes pain.

An offended friend is harder to win back than a fortified city. Arguments separate friends like a gate locked with bars.
– King Solomon –

6

NEEDS

Know her needs/-know his needs and meet them. Pay attention to your spouse's needs;-physical, sexual and emotional needs. She may want you to brush her hair. He may like when you kiss him goodbye. Sometimes it is the little things that count.

The wife does not have authority over her own body but yields it to her husband. In the same way, the husband does not have authority over his own body but yields it to his wife.
— 1 Corinthians 7:4 —

7

COMPLIMENTS

*Compliment each other, tell
her how good she looks in that
dress, and tell him what a
hunk he is in that suit.
Your compliments
create smiles.*

*How you make others feel about
themselves says a lot about you.*
– Anonymous –

8

HEALTH

*Try to stay fit and healthy.
Make an effort. to look good
and stay looking good.
Exercise together you'll either
get really fit together or laugh
really hard together.*

*Beloved, I wish above all things that
you may prosper and be in health,
even as your soul prospers*
– 3 John 1:2 –

9

MONEY

*Never argue about money,
Money comes and money
goes, but never argue about it
and never hide it from one
another. You are now joined
together as one in Holy
matrimony. The wife's money
is now the husband money
and the husband's money is
now the wife's.*

*And my God will supply every need of yours
according to his riches in glory in Christ Jesus.*
– Philippians 4:9 –

10

AGREEMENT

Be in agreement about your goals, financial goals, business goals, family goals, make sure you both know each others goals and do everything you can to help each other reach those goals.

Can two people walk together without agreeing on the direction?
– Amos 3:3 –

11

WORDS

*Do not speak harmful and
hurtful things to each other,
People never forget words
that are spoken, death and life
are in the power of the words
we speak. They have the
power to build up and they
have the power to tear down.*

*Does anyone want to live a life
that is long and prosperous?
Then keep your tongue from speaking evil
and your lips from telling lies!*
– Kind David –

12

LISTEN

Pay attention to what your spouse says, they will usually speak what they feel. Also be aware of the unspoken conversations and the deafening silence that may come from your spouse, it's a sign something is wrong. Don't leave it, fix it.

The Word LISTEN contains the same letters as the word SILENT.
– Alfred Brendel –

13

SEX

Yes it's very important, discuss what you both need and like. Schedule the time and don't leave long periods of abstinence. It's not healthy and this can lead to grumpy spouse.

Sex will fall by the wayside if you do not intentionally make it a priority.
– One Flesh Marriage with Brad & Kate –

14

HOUSEWORK

Find out what works for you as a couple, Some women are happy with being in charge of the house work, that's their department they like to cook, clean and do not want it any other way. Some prefer to share the labour. Discuss (early on in your marriage, or before) what works best for you both. Nothing drains a marriage like a tired spouse who gets no help in raising children, school, cleaning, housework, etc, etc.

Housework is what a woman does that nobody notices unless she hasn't done it.
– Evan Esar –

15

FAMILY

*Never bad mouth each other,
Or each others mother in
laws, you may laugh but it
still happens, don't do it,
your spouse probably already
knows their parents short
comings.*

*Learn to respect, appreciate and celebrate your
mother and father in law, after all they're the
reason you have the wonderful partner.*
– Kevin Treasure –

16

EYES

Don't look at anything that does not belong in your future, other women, other + men are exactly that-others, Don't look to long, looks can quickly turns to lust, which leads to desire which creates a need, which you will eventually want to fulfil. It will all end in regret. Safety first, Keep your head straight and keep walking.

I made a covenant with my eyes, how then should I look lustfully at a young woman?
– Job 31:1 –

17

ROMANCE

Keep it alive, some couples make all the effort before marriage to wine and dine their partners and when they get married they whine and die. Once the marriage has started, romance, flowers, dinner, all goes out the window and is forgotten about. Make every effort to keep your loving new.

Keep the fire lit in your marriage and your life will be filled with warmth.
– Fawn Weaver –

18

SURPRISE

Surprise one another, do spur of the moment things, which add spice to your marriage. We are going out, tonight, I have arranged a dinner, theatre, etc (Always check calendars and arrange babysitters before this point)

A great illusion is that love is self-sustaining. Love must be fed and nurtured

19

WORK

Men should posses a strong desire to support their family, but never let your job or business take president over your marriage. It will be the beginning of the end for your marriage.

A 'good job' can be both practically attractive while still not good enough to devote your entire life to.
– Alain de Botton –

20

AVOID

*Doing things you know your
spouse does not like, if it
makes her upset, don't do it.
Its not rocket science, if he
does not like it, make a mental
note and avoid it.*

*Committing to staying calm is the first key
to committing to staying married.*
– Hal Runkel –

21

ENCOURAGE

Encourage each other in each others strengths; stop pointing out each others weaknesses. Focus on each others gifts, talents and strengths.

Be presidents of each other's fan clubs.
— Tony Heath —

22

INTEREST

Have a common interest as well as your own, learn to share your interest, be interested in the things your spouse is interested in. You never know she may like football, and he may like the theatre. (We live in hope)

Real giving is when we give to our spouses what's important to them, whether we understand it, like it, agree with it, or not.
– Michele Weiner-Davis –

23

TIME

Have a night in, rent a movie, get some popcorn, and send the kids to grandparents and TURN OFF THE MOBILE PHONE, One thing you cannot get back is time, Use it well.

A newly married man must not be drafted into the army or be given any other official responsibilities. He must be free to spend one year at home, bringing happiness to the wife he has married.
– Deuteronomy 24:5 –

24

PAST

Is exactly that, the past, leave things in the past and resist temptation to bring things up that happened six years ago. It only generates more strife.

One day you'll find someone who doesn't care about your past because they want to be your future.
– Unknown –

25

AFFECTION

*You can still hold hands, Kiss
her goodbye and hug him
when you meet him.
Stroke her hair,
Pinch his bum.
The kids will cringe
but he will smile.*

*Let your wife be a fountain of blessing for you.
Rejoice in the wife of your youth.*
– Proverbs 5:18 –

26

LAUGH

*Remember to Laugh, It is a great medicine. Always remember to have fun and laugh. Don't take life so seriously, Find things on purpose to laugh at.
Like each other.*

It is not a lack of love, but a lack of friendship that makes unhappy marriages.

27

REMEMBER

Marriage is a God given union between a man and a woman. God is love, when you display love one towards another in your marriage you're pleasing God.

Nevertheless let every one of you in particular so love his wife even as himself; and the wife see that she reverence her husband.
– Ephesians 5:33 –

THE POWER OF
DIVINE
DIRECTION

The Winners Mentality *Series*

KEVIN A TREASURE

COMING SOON

GIMM RADIO

For the best in gospel music, preaching and teaching.

http://www.gimmradio.com

http://www.gimm.tv

Printed in Great Britain
by Amazon

33108339R00030